Cursive
HANDWRITING
PRACTICE
LEFT HANDED ADULTS

LETTERS INSPIRATIONAL WORDS QUOTES

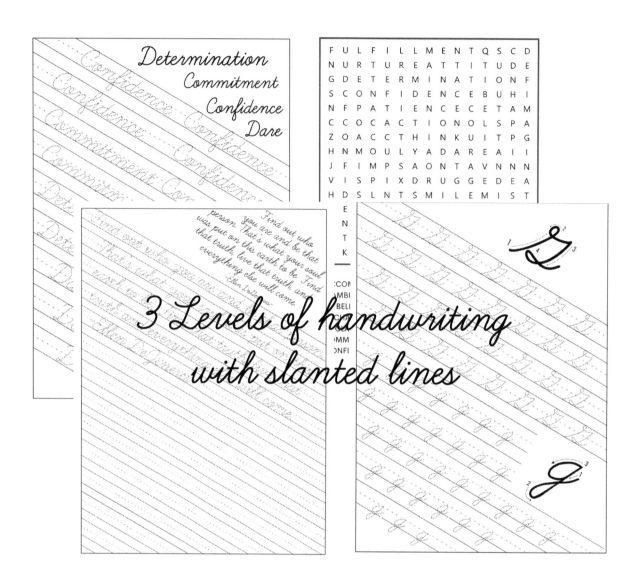

3 Levels of handwriting
with slanted lines

FOR ANY SUGGESTS OR QUESTIONS REGARDING OUR
BOOK, PLEASE CONTACT US AT :
ATNINTHDESSERT@GMAIL.COM

ISBN: 979-8407547518

A Few Helpful Tips

- Left-handed people should sit slightly to the left of the center and tilt the paper down for better visibility. Therefore, this workbook is designed with slanted lines to prevent getting caught, dirty and improve visibility without tilting.

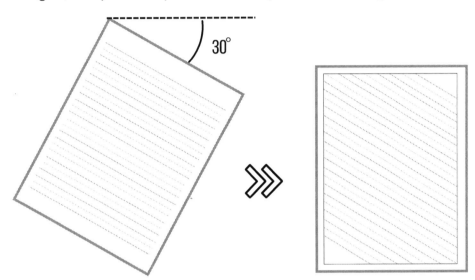

- Left-handed writers should also have enough lighting so that the shadow of your hand doesn't interfere with your writing.

- Left-handed cursive writers should use a pencil grip to hold the pencil far enough away from the tip. This allows you to better see the formation of the letters you are writing on the paper.

Cursive Alphabet Guide

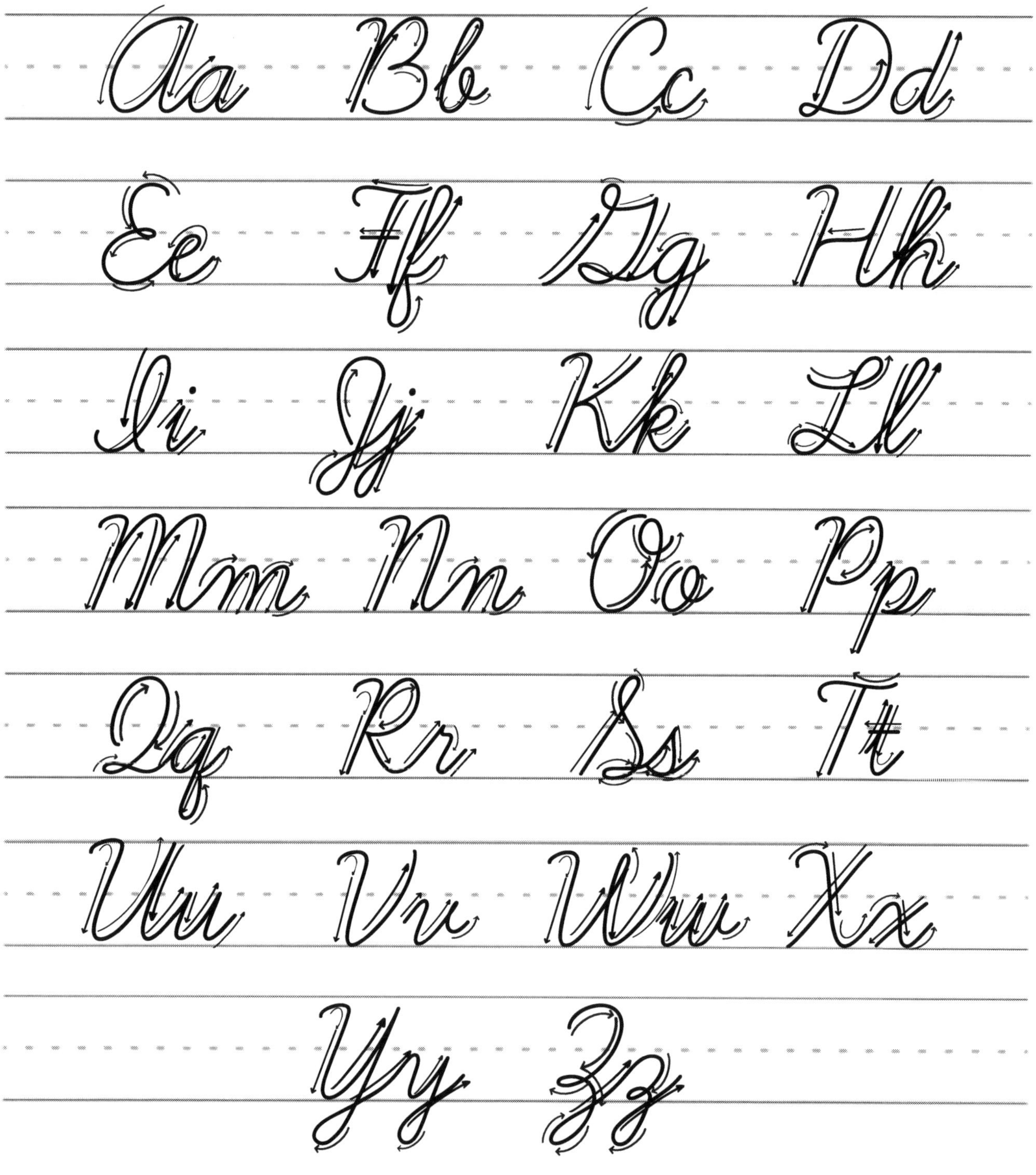

Aa Bb Cc Dd

Ee Ff Gg Hh

Ii Jj Kk Ll

Mm Nn Oo Pp

Qq Rr Ss Tt

Uu Vv Ww Xx

Yy Zz

Part 1

Letter & Number

with slanted lines

help left-handers writers from snagging and smudging the worksheet.

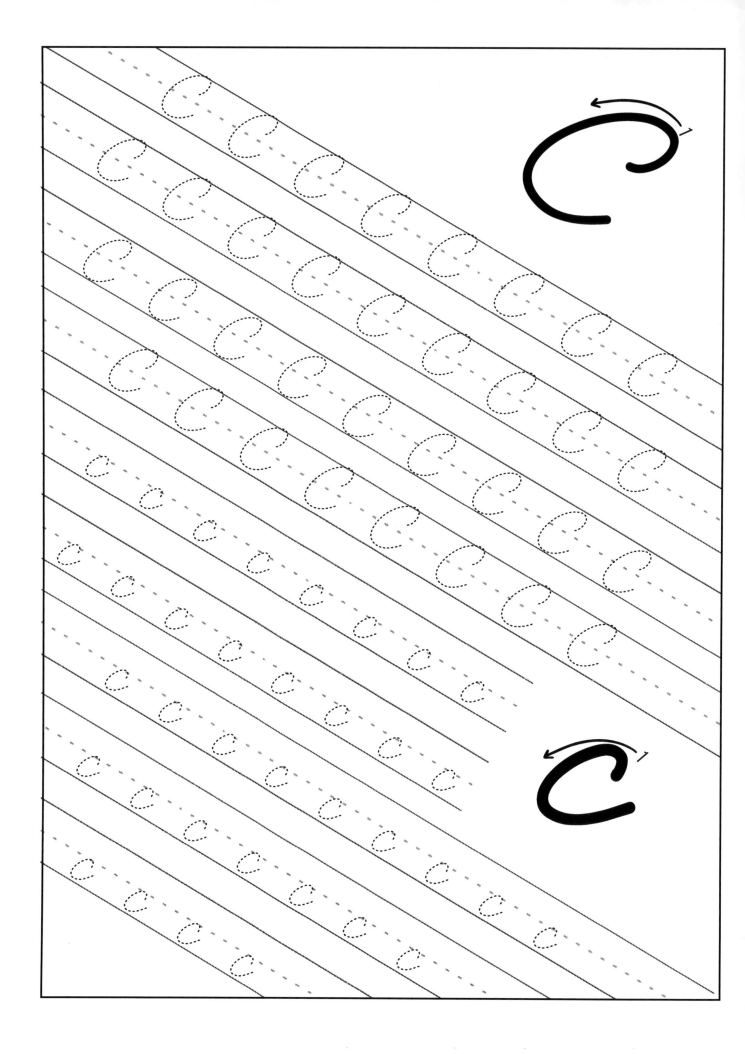

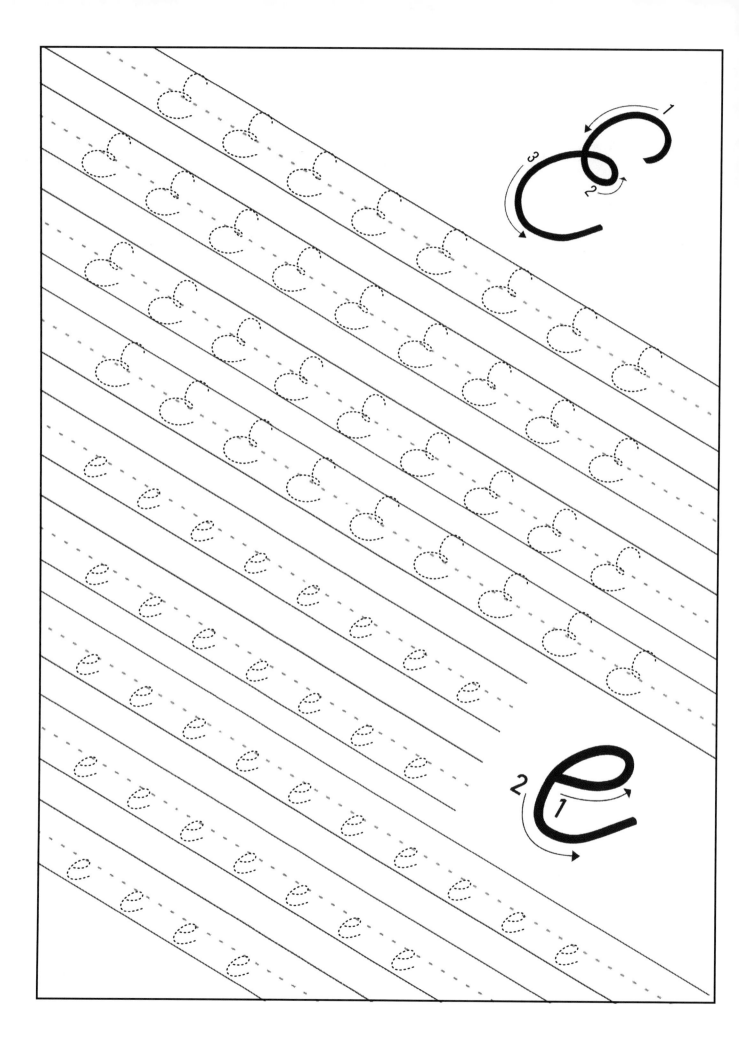

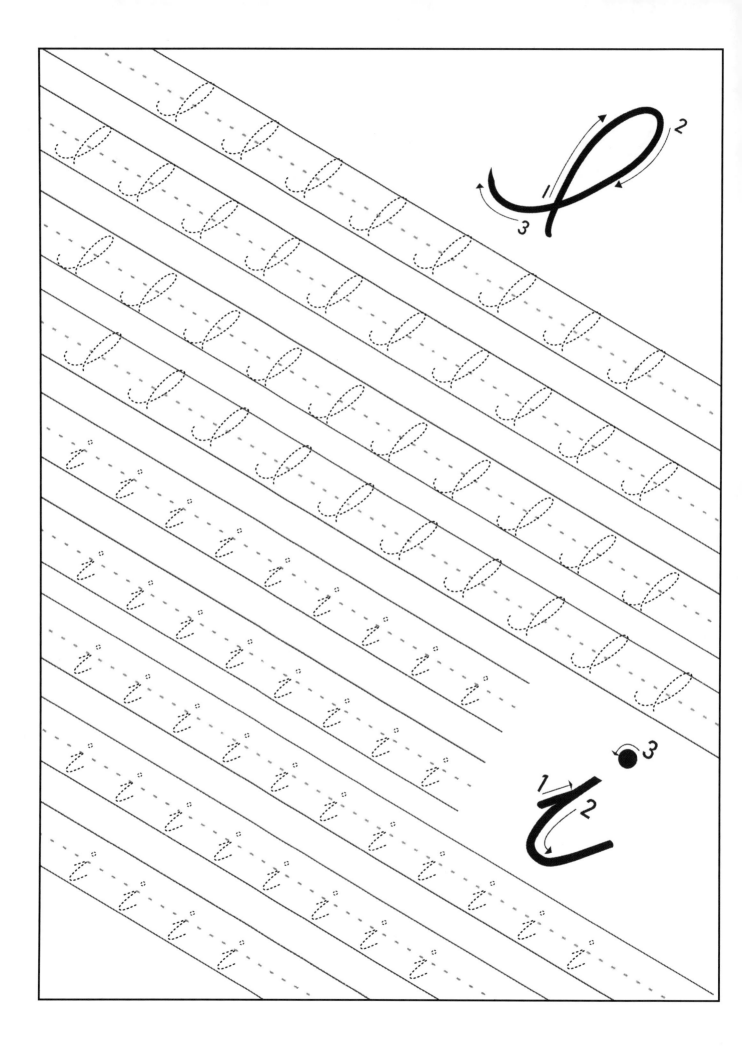

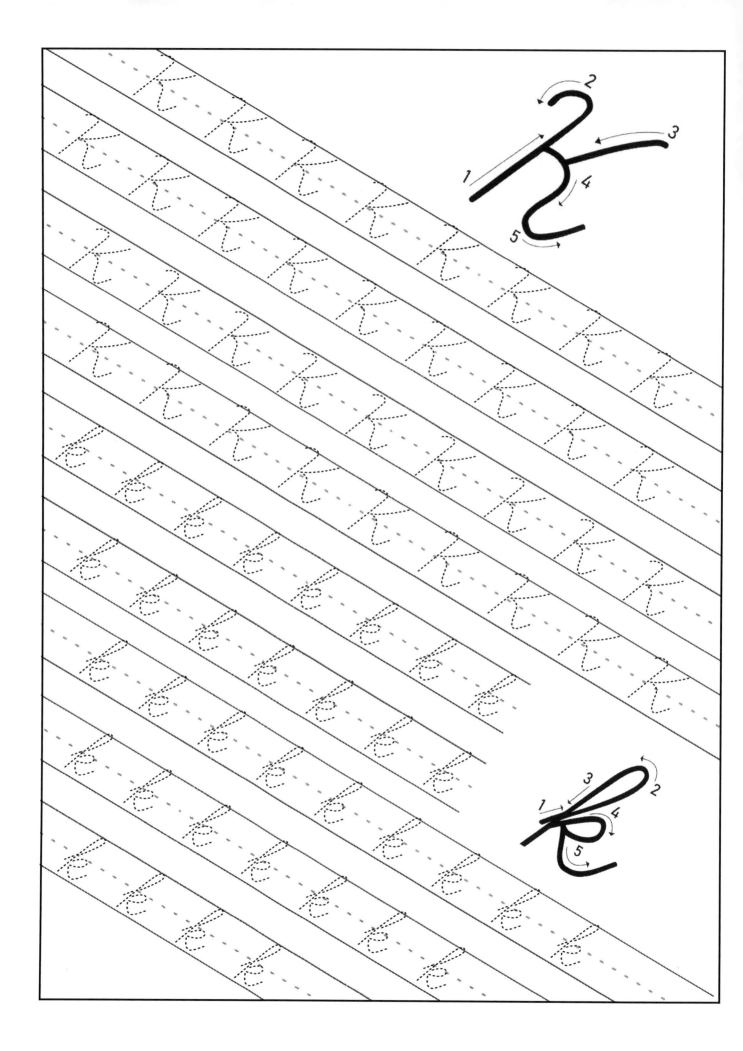

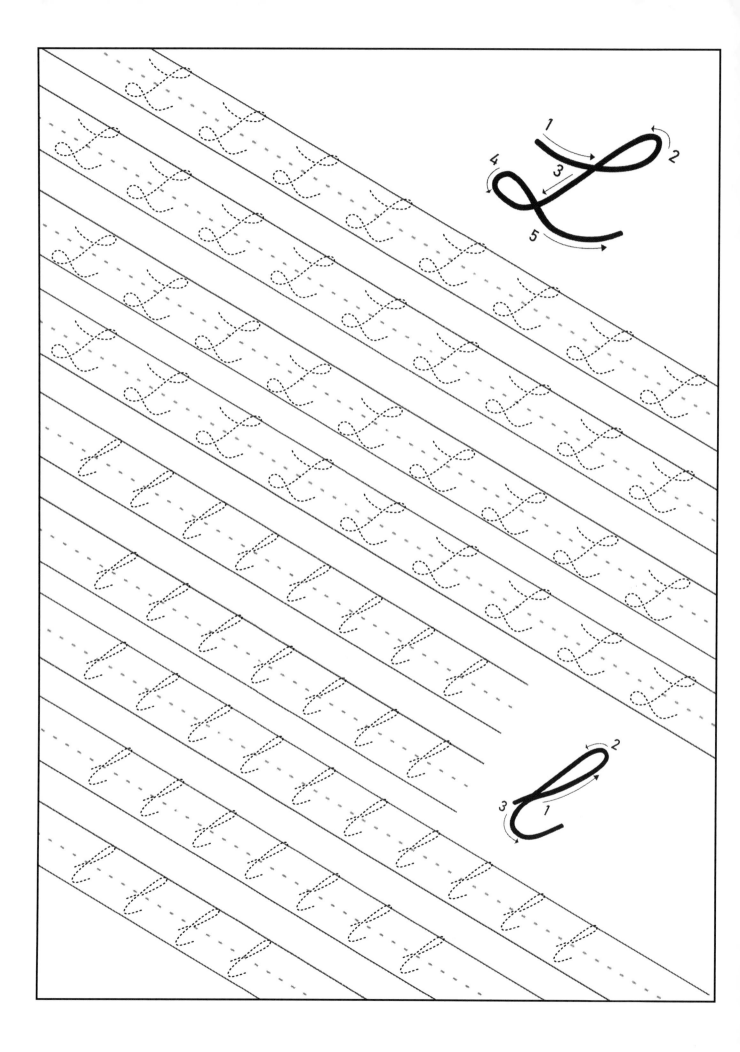

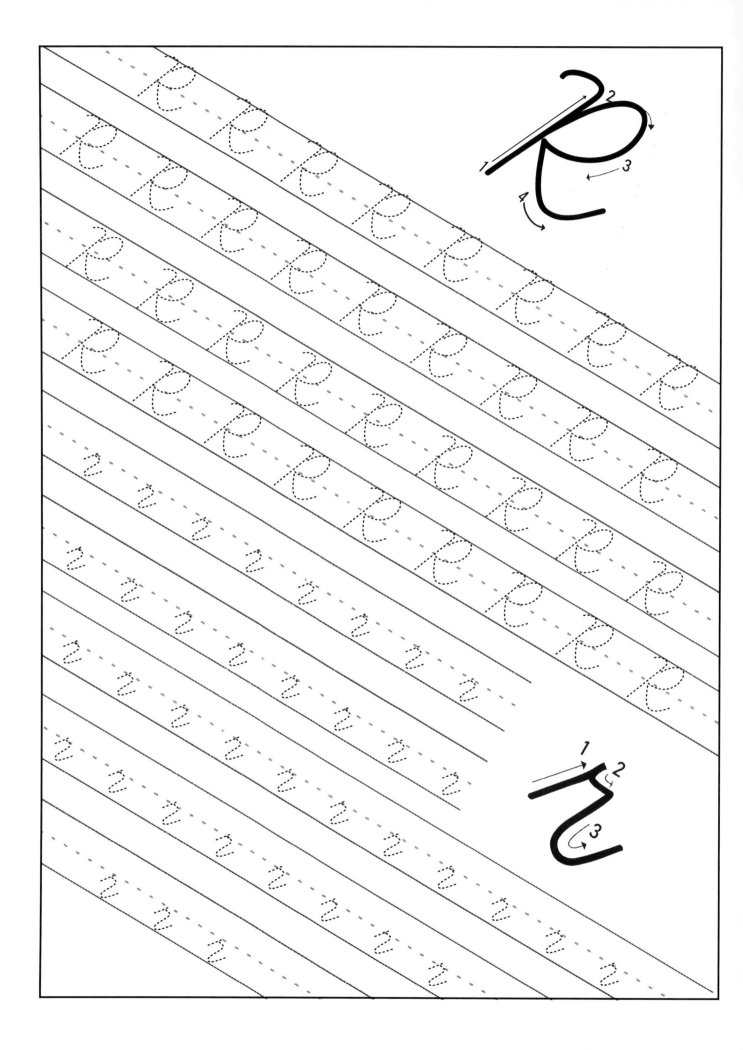

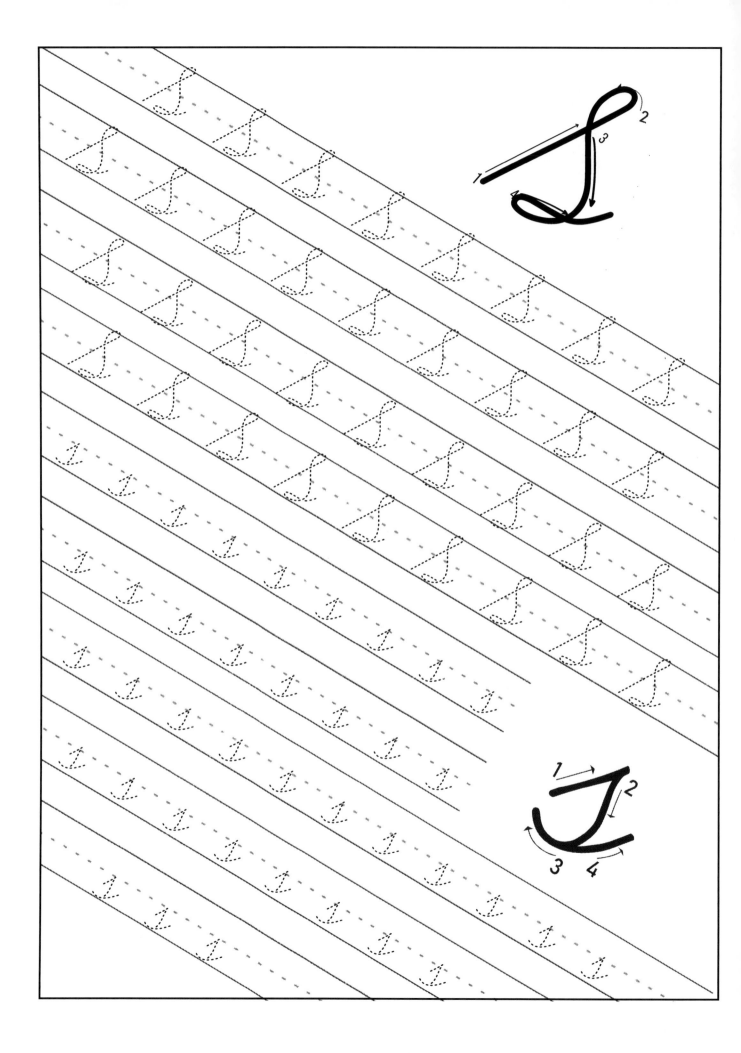

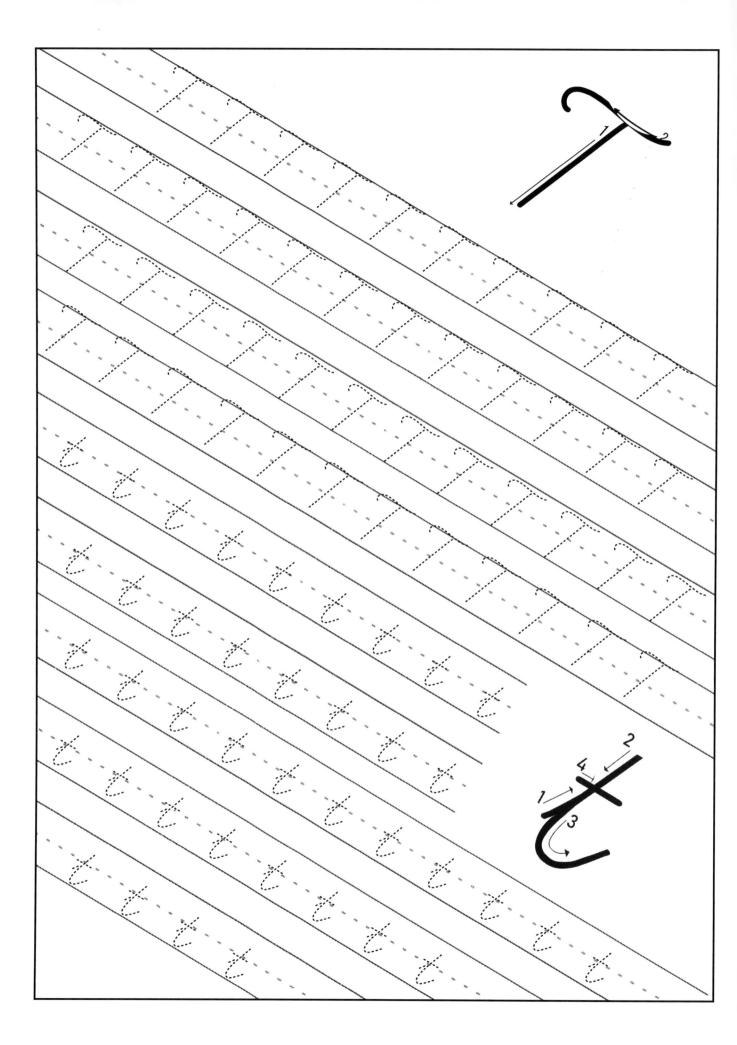

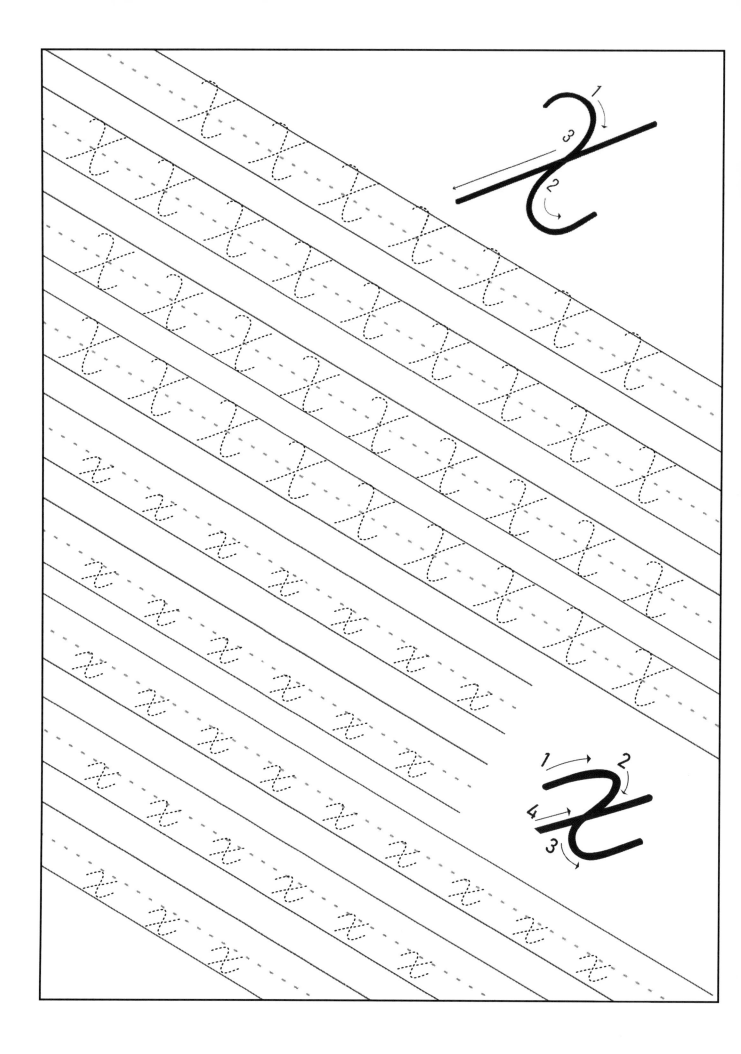

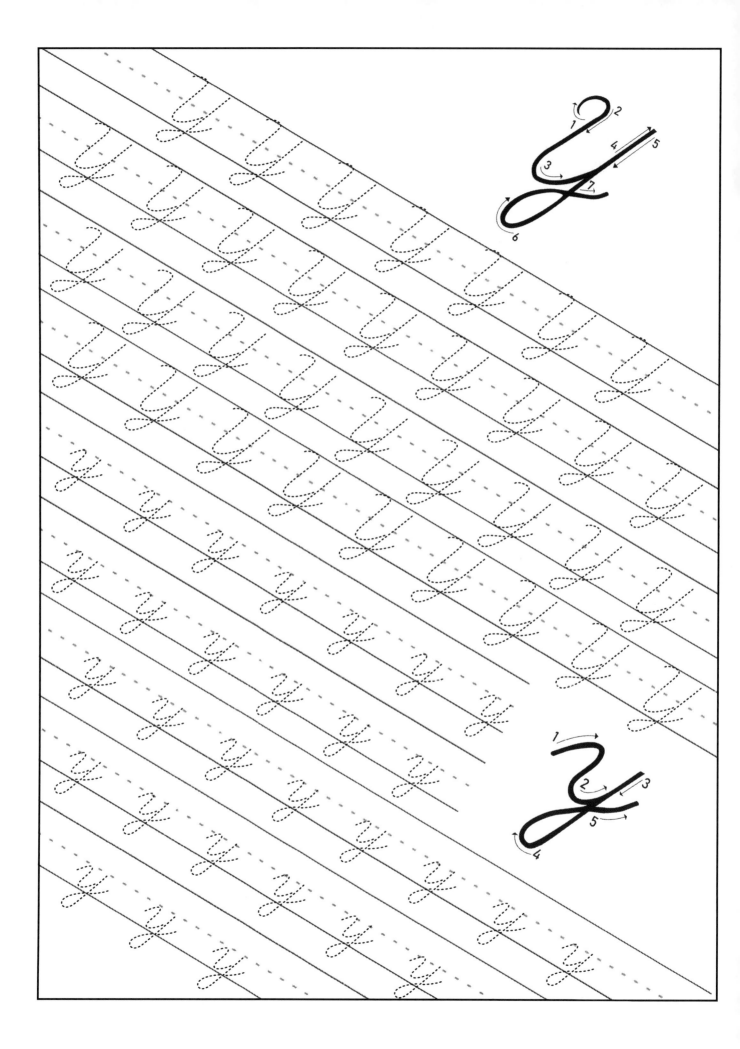

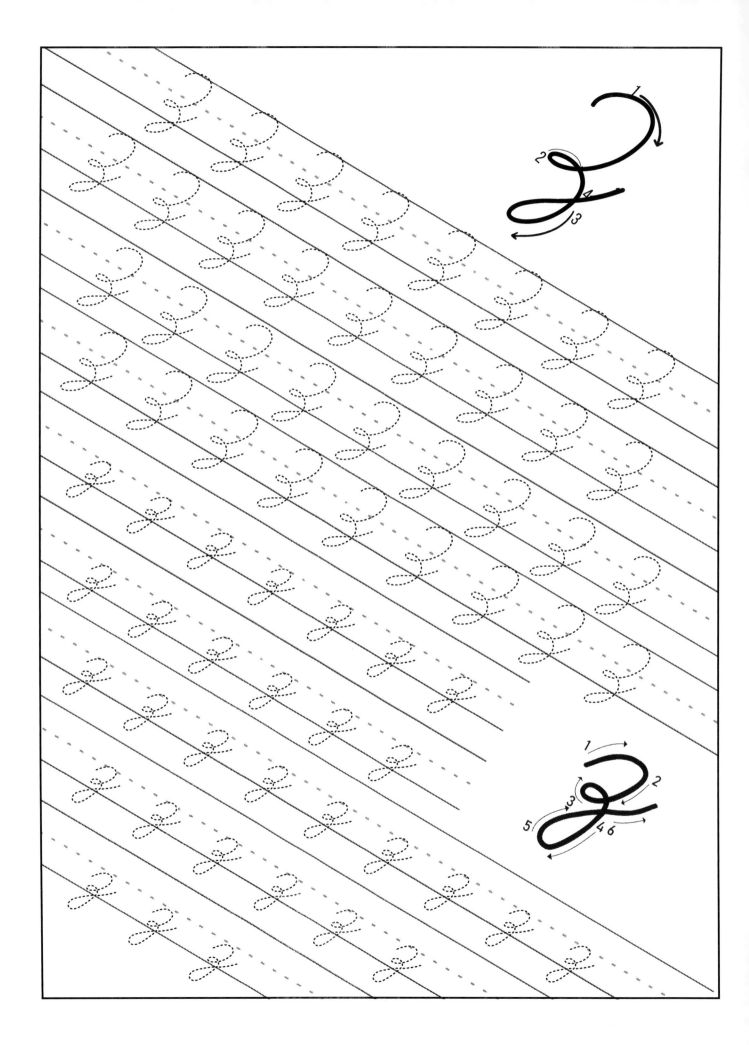

Two

Four

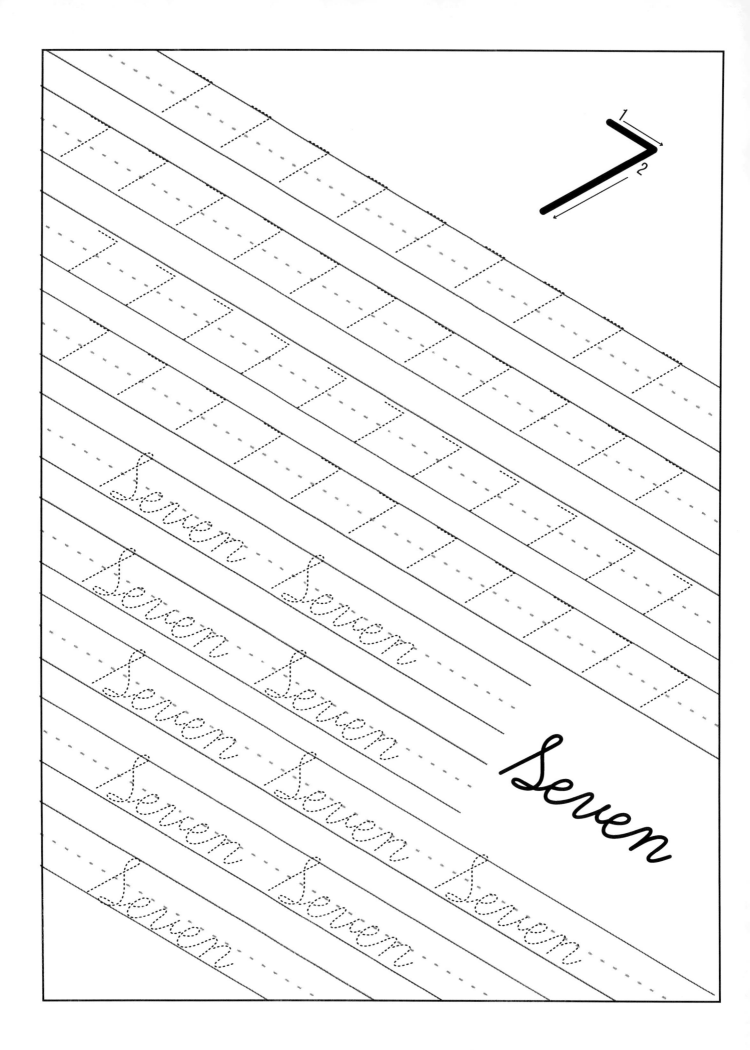

Part 2

Motivational Words Search

with slanted lines

help left-handers writers
from snagging and smudging the worksheet.

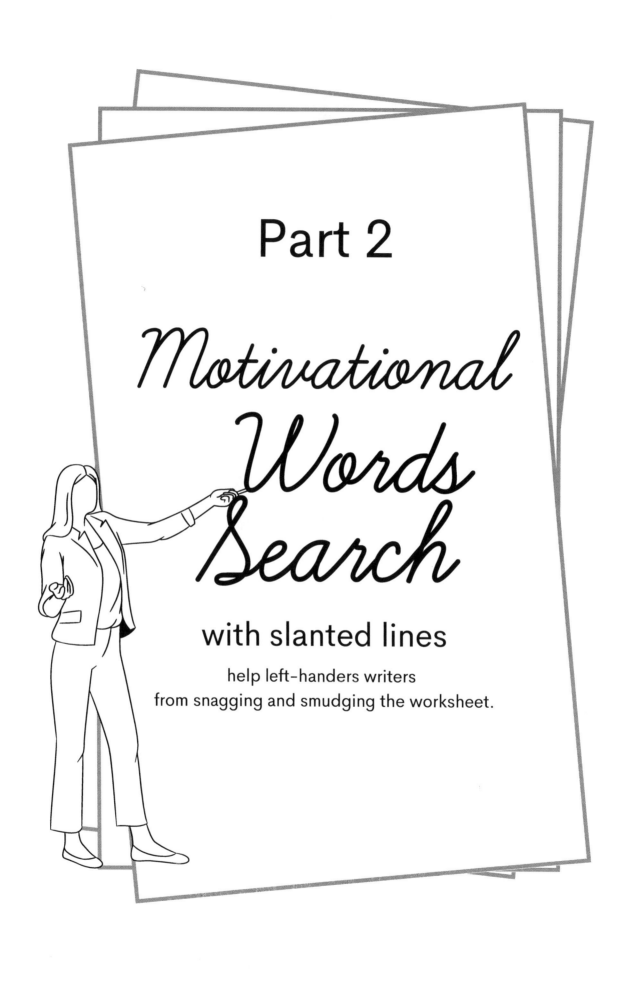

Word Search

d	c	r	u	h	e	o	d	j
r	l	c	a	n	o	b	d	n
r	e	h	t	o	m	u	u	e
d	a	h	y	r	v	a	i	o
c	v	p	t	b	w	q	s	s
n	e	t	c	a	i	l	n	e
z	h	s	e	l	f	t	c	t
o	d	s	q	l	e	e	p	s
g	b	s	b	g	e	c	n	v

ACCOMPLISH	COURAGE	HAPPINESS
AMBITION	DARE	IMAGINATION
BELIEVE	DETERMINATION	MISSION
CHANGE	ENVISION	NURTURE
CLARITY	FOCUS	OUTSTANDING
COMMITMENT	FULFILLMENT	PATIENCE
CONFIDENCE	GRATITUDE	

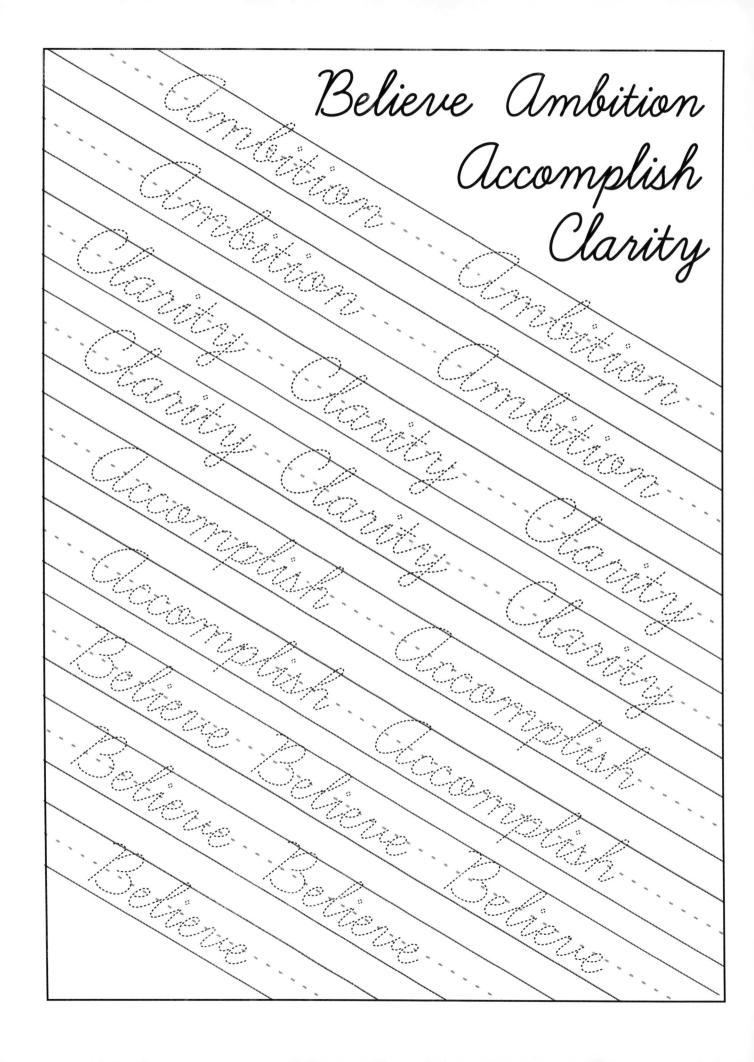

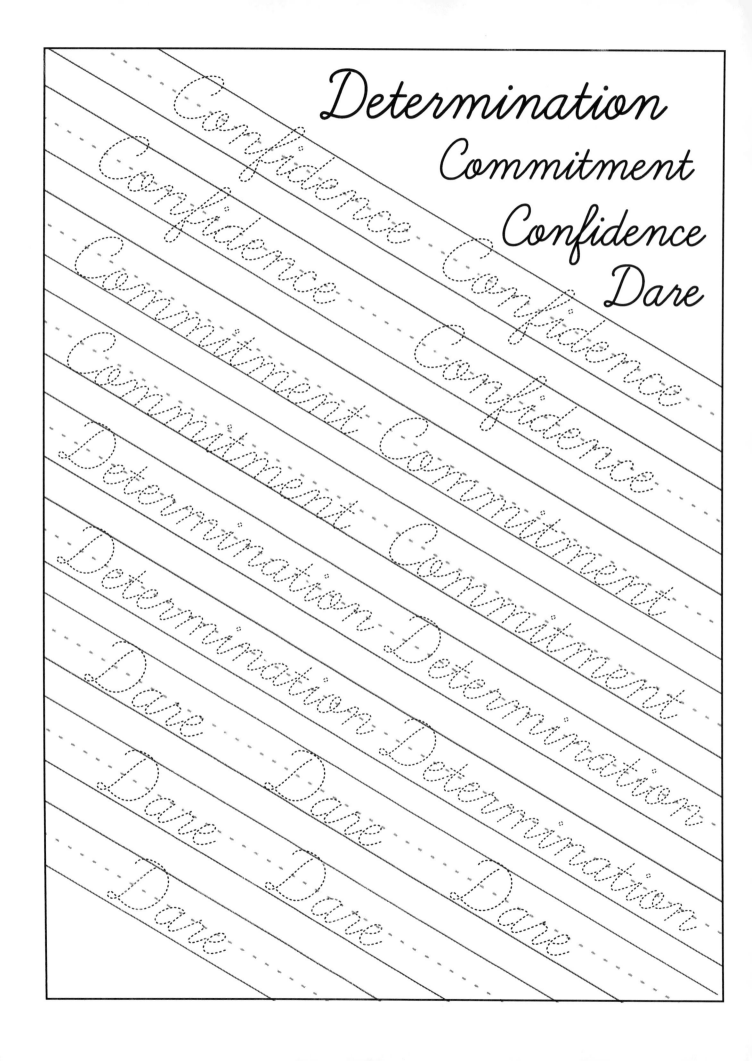

Determination
Commitment
Confidence
Dare

Date

Commitment

Determination

Confidence

Fulfillment
Happiness
Envision
Focus

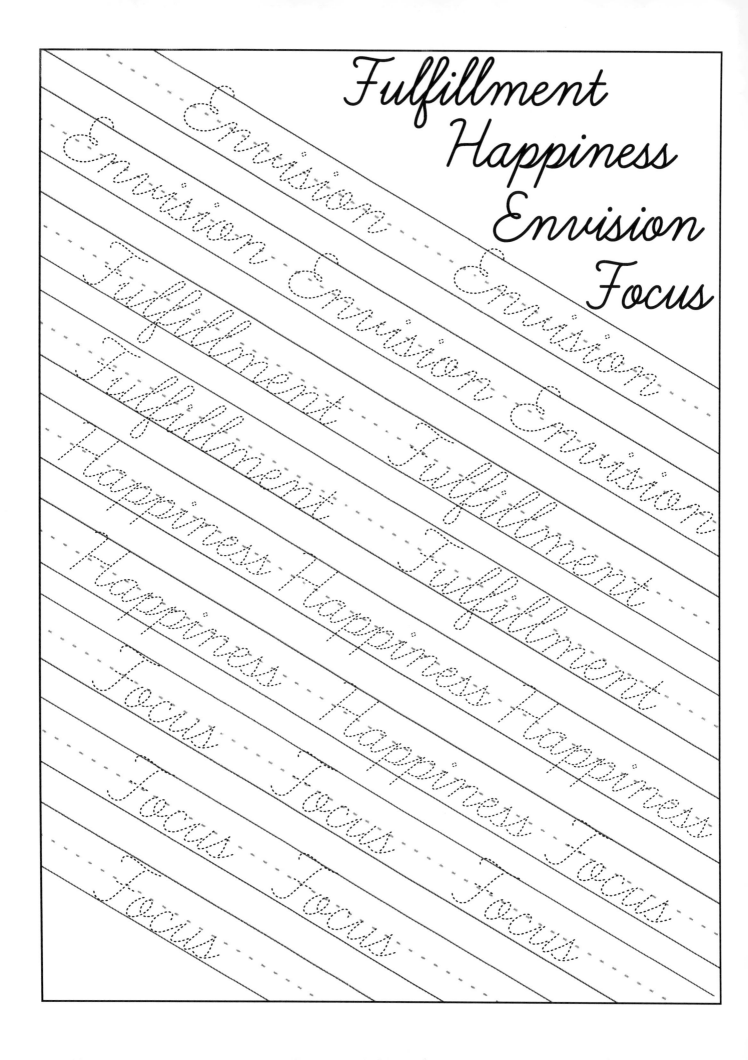

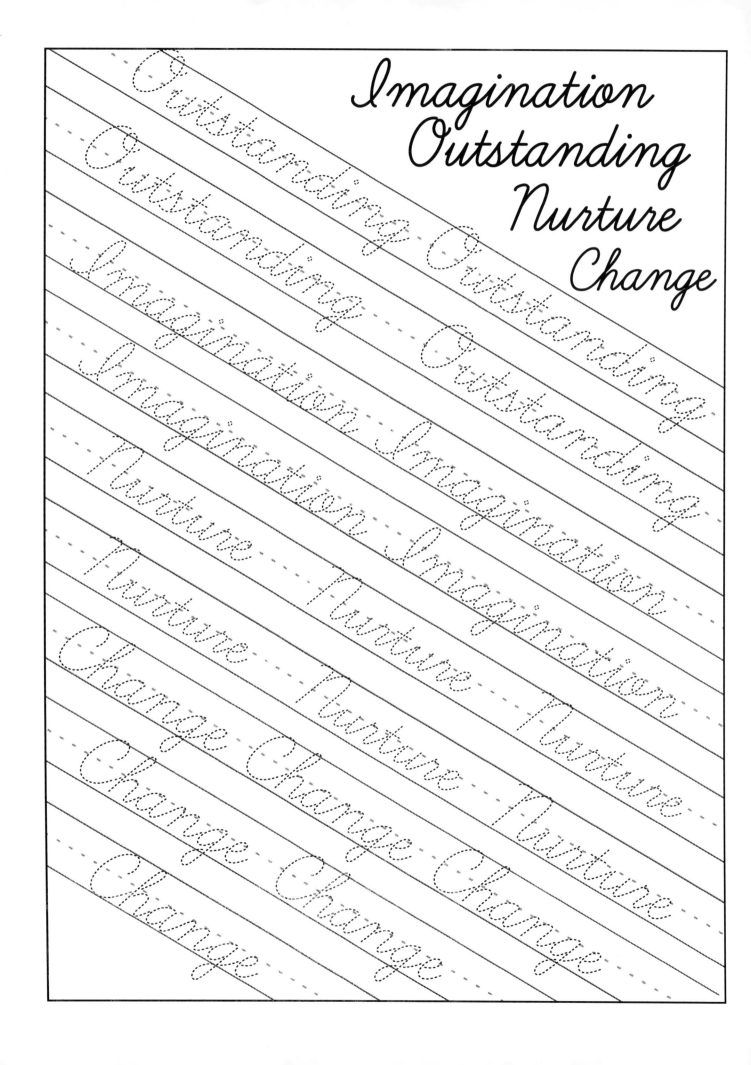

Imagination
Outstanding
Nurture
Change

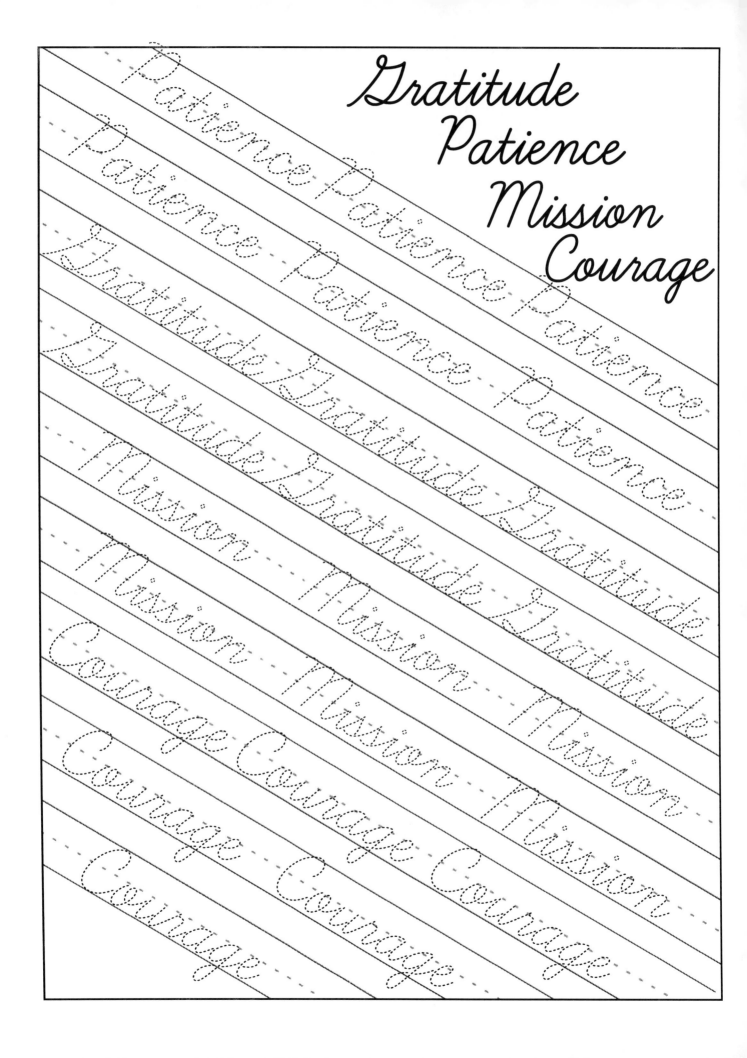

Gratitude
Patience
Mission
Courage

Part 3

Motivational *Quotes*

with slanted lines

help left-handers writers
from snagging and smudging
the worksheet.

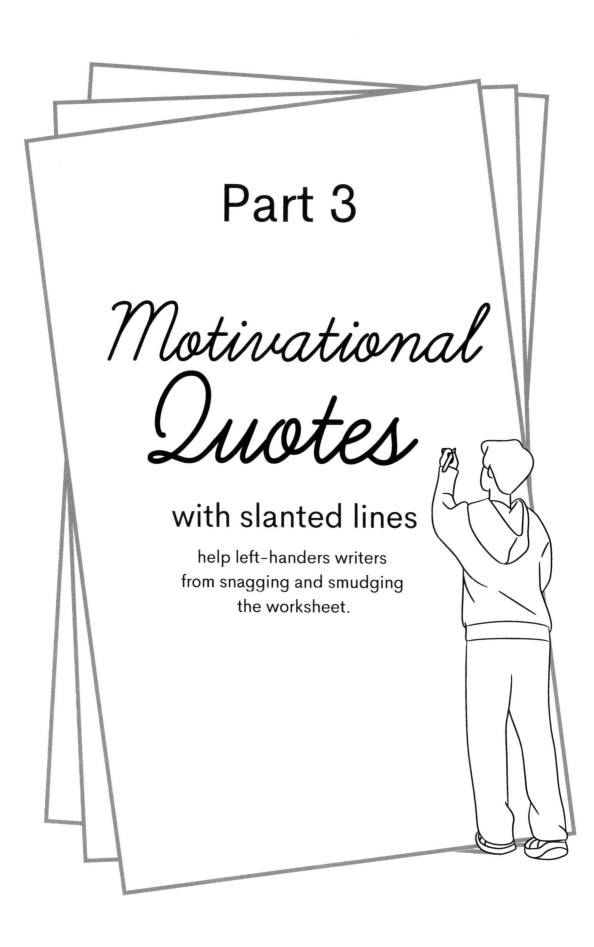

You can do anything as long as you have the passion, the drive, the focus, and the support.

— Sabrina Bryan —

You can do anything as long as you have the passion, the drive, the focus, and the support.

— Sabrina Bryan —

and the support.

have the passion, the drive, the focus

You can do anything as long as you

"Believe it can be done. When you believe something can be done, really believe, your mind will find the ways to do it. Believing a solution paves the way to solution."

—David Joseph Schwartz—

Believe it can be done. When you believe, something can be done, really believe, your mind will find the ways to do it. Believing a solution paves the way to solution. —David Joseph Schwartz

The mind is. As long as
the limit. As long as the fact
the mind can envision the fact
that you can do something, you
can do it, as long as you really believe
100 percent.

— Arnold Schwarzenegger —

The mind is the limit. As long as you can do
something you can do it as long as you really
mind can do it as you can do
something you can do it.

Arnold Schwarzenegger

believe 100 percent.

Find out who
you are and be that
person. That's what your soul
was put on this earth to be. Find
that truth, live that truth, and
everything else will come.
-Ellen DeGeneres-

Find out who you are and be that person.
That's what your soul was put on this
earth to be. Find that truth, live that
truth and everything else will come.
-Ellen DeGeneres-

If you nurture and
your mind, body; and
spirit, your time will expand.
You will gain a new perspective
that will allow you to accomplish
much more.
— Brian Koslow —

If you nurture your mind, body;
and spirit, your time will expand. You
will gain a new perspective that will allow you
to accomplish much more.
— Brian Koslow —

Made in the USA
Las Vegas, NV
09 January 2024

84101251R00059